WEEKLY TORAH PORTION

Activity Book

Weekly Torah Portion Activity Book

Bible Pathway Adventures® is a trademark of BPA Publishing Ltd.
Defenders of the Faith® is a trademark of BPA Publishing Ltd.

ISBN: 978-1-98-858530-7

Author: Pip Reid
Creative Director: Curtis Reid

For more Bible resources, including Activity Books and printables, visit our website at:

www.biblepathwayadventures.com

◦◇ **Introduction** ◇◦

joy teaching your children about the Torah with our *Weekly Torah Portion Activity ook*. Packed with 54 coloring worksheets, five weekly Torah study guides, and a Parsha otes activity page to help educators just like you teach children a Biblical faith. The erfect discipleship resource for Sabbath lessons and homeschooling. Includes scripture ferences for easy Bible verse look-up, and a handy answer key for teachers and rents.

ble Pathway Adventures helps educators teach children the Biblical faith in a fun and eative way. We do this via our free printables, illustrated Bible storybooks, and Activity ooks. Learn more at: www.biblepathwayadventures.com

hanks for buying this Activity Book and supporting our ministry. Every book purchased lps us continue our work providing Classroom Packs and discipleship resources to milies and missions around the world.

The search for Truth is more fun than Tradition!

◇ Table of Contents ◇

© BPA Publishing Ltd 2020

Bereshit

Read Genesis 1:1-6:8. Write a summary of this Torah Portion.

1. On which day did Yah create man?

2. Who named all the animals?

3. How old was Adam when he died?

Draw your favorite scene from this Torah Portion.

Yah used Adam & Eve to…

This Torah Portion teaches me…

Noach

ad Genesis 6:9-11:32. Write a summary of this Torah Portion.

....

....

....

1. How many pairs of each 'clean' animal were on the ark?

....

....

2. What was the sign of a covenant between Yah and Noah?

....

....

3. How high did the people want to build the tower of Babel?

....

Draw your favorite scene from this Torah Portion.

Yah used Noah to…	This Torah Portion teaches me…

Lech-Lecha

Read Genesis 12:1-17:27. Write a summary of this Torah Portion.

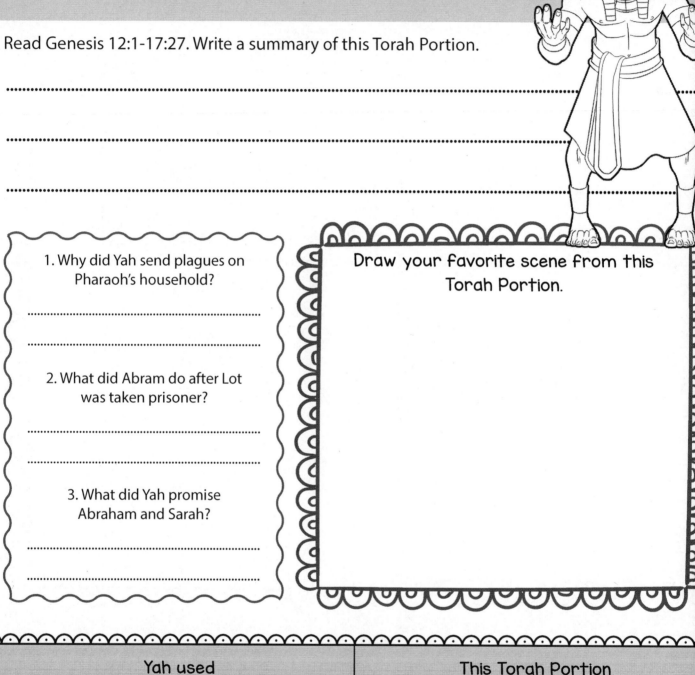

1. Why did Yah send plagues on Pharaoh's household?

2. What did Abram do after Lot was taken prisoner?

3. What did Yah promise Abraham and Sarah?

Draw your favorite scene from this Torah Portion.

Yah used Abraham to…

This Torah Portion teaches me…

Vayeira

ad Genesis 18:1-22:24. Write a summary of this Torah Portion.

....

....

....

1. Who was Abraham's wife?

....

....

2. What rained down on Sodom and Gomorrah?

....

....

3. Why did Abraham take his son to the land of Moriah?

....

....

Draw your favorite scene from this Torah Portion.

What could I learn from the life of Abraham?	This Torah Portion teaches me…

Chayei Sarah

Read Genesis 23:1-25:18. Write a summary of this Torah Portion.

....

....

....

1. Where did Abraham bury Sarah?

....

....

2. What gifts did the servant give Rebekah?

....

....

3. Who did Rebekah marry when she arrived in the Negeb?

....

....

Draw your favorite scene from this Torah Portion.

Yah used the servant to…

This Torah Portion teaches me…

....

....

....

....

Toledot

Read Genesis 25:19-28:9. Write a summary of this Torah Portion.

....

....

....

1. Who were Isaac and Rebekah's twin sons?

....

....

2. Why did the Philistines envy Isaac?

....

....

3. Why did Jacob flee to Paddan-aram and live with Laban?

....

....

Draw your favorite scene from this Torah Portion.

Yah used Isaac to…	This Torah Portion teaches me…
....	....
....	....

Vayetze

Read Genesis 28:10-32:3. Write a summary of this Torah Portion.

....

....

....

1. Who was on the ladder in Jacob's dream?

....

....

2. How many years did Jacob work for Rachel?

....

....

3. Where did Rachel hide her father's household gods?

....

....

Draw your favorite scene from this Torah Portion.

Yah used Jacob to...

....

....

This Torah Portion teaches me...

....

....

Vayishlach

ad Genesis 32:4-36:43. Write a summary of this Torah Portion.

....

....

....

1. How many men did Esau bring with him to see Jacob?

....

....

2. Why did Yah change Jacob's name to Israel?

....

....

3. Why did Esau move his family to the hill country of Seir?

....

....

Draw your favorite scene from this Torah Portion.

List the gifts that Jacob got ready for Esau.

....

....

This Torah Portion teaches me...

....

....

Vayeshev

Read Genesis 37:1-40:24. Write a summary of this Torah Portion.

....

....

....

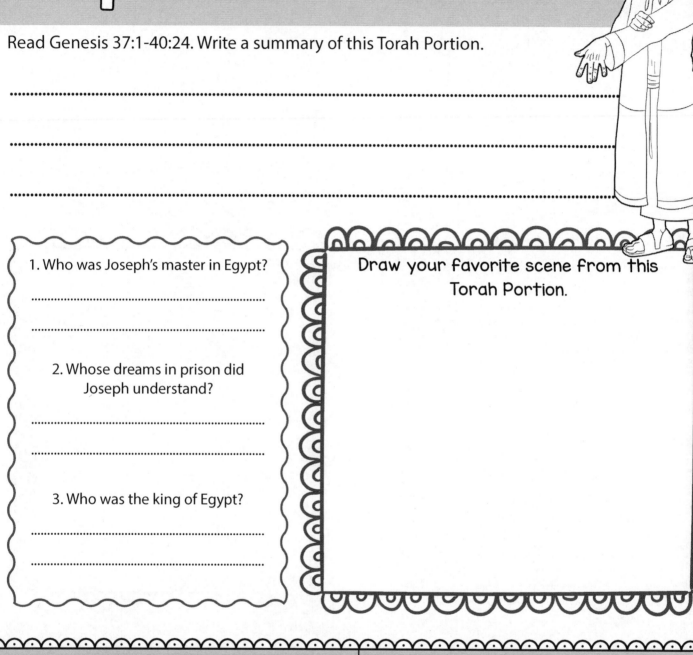

1. Who was Joseph's master in Egypt?

....

....

2. Whose dreams in prison did Joseph understand?

....

....

3. Who was the king of Egypt?

....

....

Draw your favorite scene from this Torah Portion.

Yah used
Pharaoh to…

This Torah Portion
teaches me…

....

....

....

....

Miketz

ad Genesis 41:1-44:17. Write a summary of this Torah Portion.

....

....

....

1. What new job did Pharaoh give Joseph?

....

....

2. Why did Jacob send his sons to Egypt?

....

....

3. What did Joseph tell his servant to hide in Benjamin's sack?

....

Draw your favorite scene from this Torah Portion.

List three countries that border modern-day Egypt.

This Torah Portion teaches me…

....

....

....

....

Vayigash

Read Genesis 44:18-47:27. Write a summary of this Torah Portion.

....

....

....

1. What did Pharaoh say he would give Joseph's brothers?

....

....

2. In which land did Joseph's family settle?

....

....

3. What did Joseph give the Egyptians in exchange for their livestock?

....

....

Draw your favorite scene from this Torah Portion.

Yah used Joseph to...

....

....

This Torah Portion teaches me...

....

....

Vayechi

ad Genesis 47:28-50:26. Write a summary of this Torah Portion.

....

....

....

1. Who was Joseph's firstborn son?

....

....

2. Which tribe of Israel shall be like strong donkeys?

....

....

3. How many days did the Egyptians weep for Jacob?

....

....

Draw your favorite scene from this Torah Portion.

List the twelve tribes of Israel.	This Torah Portion teaches me...

Shemot

Read Exodus 1:1-6:1. Write a summary of this Torah Portion.

....

....

....

1. What instructions did Pharaoh give the Hebrew midwives?

....

....

2. To which land did Moses flee?

....

....

3. What did Pharaoh do when Moses asked to free the Hebrews?

....

....

Draw your favorite scene from this Torah Portion.

Yah used
the midwives to…

....

....

This Torah Portion
teaches me…

....

....

Va'eira

Read Exodus 6:2-9:35. Write a summary of this Torah Portion.

....

....

....

1. With whom did Yah establish His Covenant?

....

....

2. Whose livestock died in the fifth plague?

....

....

3. In which part of Egypt did hailstones not fall?

....

....

Draw your favorite scene from this Torah Portion.

Yah used the plagues to show the Egyptians…

This Torah Portion teaches me…

....

....

Bo

Read Exodus 10:1-13:16. Write a summary of this Torah Portion.

....

....

....

1. In which Hebrew month is the Passover?

....

....

2. How long did Yah ask the Israelites to honor the Passover?

....

....

3. What was the tenth plague?

....

....

Draw your favorite scene from this Torah Portion.

Yah used the Egyptians to…

....

....

This Torah Portion teaches me…

....

....

Beshalach

Read Exodus 13:17-17:16. Write a summary of this Torah Portion.

....

....

....

1. Whose bones did the Israelites take with them?

....

....

2. How did Yah part the Red Sea?

....

....

3. How did Yah give the Israelites water at Rephidim?

....

....

Draw your favorite scene from this Torah Portion.

Yah used Joshua to…	This Torah Portion teaches me…

Yitro

Read Exodus 18:1-20:26. Write a summary of this Torah Portion.

....

....

....

1. What relation was Jethro to Moses?

....

....

2. Where were the Israelites given the Ten Commandments?

....

....

3. Which day is holy and set-apart for Yah?

....

....

Draw your favorite scene from this Torah Portion.

Yah used Jethro to…

....

....

This Torah Portion teaches me…

....

....

Mishpatim

ad Exodus 21:1-24:18. Write a summary of this Torah Portion.

....

....

....

1. What should happen to the land every seventh year?

....

....

2. What type of bread is eaten during Unleavened Bread?

....

....

3. On which three Feasts should males appear before Yah?

....

....

Draw your favorite scene from this Torah Portion.

Yah asks us to honor the Sabbath because…	This Torah Portion teaches me…
....	....
....	....

Terumah

Read Exodus 25:1-27:19. Write a summary of this Torah Portion.

....

....

....

1. What type of wood was used to make the Ark?

....

....

2. What did Yah say to place inside the Ark?

....

....

3. What metal was used to make the mercy seat?

....

....

Draw your favorite scene from this Torah Portion.

Obeying Yah's commandments helps me..

....

....

This Torah Portion teaches me...

....

....

Tetzaveh

ad Exodus 27:20-30:10. Write a summary of this Torah Portion.

....

....

....

1. Which three men did Yah choose to serve as priests?

....

....

2. How many stones were on the High Priest's breastplate?

....

....

3. What color was the robe of the ephod?

....

....

Draw your favorite scene from this Torah Portion.

Yah used the High Priest to…	This Torah Portion teaches me…
....	....
....	....

Ki Tisa

Read Exodus 30:11-34:35. Write a summary of this Torah Portion.

....

....

....

1. What animal did Aaron make out of gold?

....

....

2. How did Moses destroy the golden calf?

....

....

3. How did Moses punish the Israelites for worshiping the calf?

....

....

Draw your favorite scene from this Torah Portion.

Yah used Bezaleel and Oholiab to…

....

....

This Torah Portion teaches me…

....

....

Vayakhel

...ad Exodus 35:1-38:20. Write a summary of this Torah Portion.

....

....

....

1. What type of craftsman were chosen to make the Tabernacle?

....

....

2. How many branches are on the menorah?

....

....

3. What metal was used to make the tent pegs?

....

....

Draw your favorite scene from this Torah Portion.

I give generously to Yah by...

....

....

This Torah Portion teaches me...

....

....

Pekudei

Read Exodus 38:21-40:38. Write a summary of this Torah Portion.

....

....

....

1. How much gold was used to build the sanctuary?

....

....

2. Where did Moses put the altar of burnt offering?

....

....

3. What was on the Tabernacle by day and by night?

....

....

Draw your favorite scene from this Torah Portion.

How would you describe Bezaleel's character?

....

....

This Torah Portion teaches me…

....

....

Vayikra

ad Leviticus 1:1-5:26 (6:7). Write a summary of this Torah Portion.

....

....

....

1. Where did the Israelites bring their burnt offering?

....

....

2. What type of birds were used as burnt offerings?

....

....

3. What animal was killed as a sin offering for a priest?

....

....

Draw your favorite scene from this Torah Portion.

The priests made offerings to…	This Torah Portion teaches me…
....	....
....	....

Tzav

Read Leviticus 6:8-8:36. Write a summary of this Torah Portion.

....

....

....

1. Who may eat the sin offering?

....

....

2. Where did the Israelites watch Moses anoint Aaron and his sons?

....

....

3. What did Moses place in the breastpiece?

....

....

Draw your favorite scene from this Torah Portion.

Yah used
the priests to…

This Torah Portion
teaches me…

....

....

Shemini

Read Leviticus 9:1-11:47. Write a summary of this Torah Portion.

....

....

....

1. Who were the two sons of Aaron?

....

....

2. What did Aaron's sons offer before Yah?

....

....

3. How did Aaron's sons die?

....

....

Draw your favorite scene from this Torah Portion.

It's important to obey Yah's instructions because…	This Torah Portion teaches me…
....	....
....	....

Tazria

Read Leviticus 12:1-13:59. Write a summary of this Torah Portion.

....

....

....

1. Who examines a person with leprosy?

....

....

2. What clothing does a leprous man wear?

....

....

3. Where does a leprous man live while he is unclean?

....

....

Draw your favorite scene from this Torah Portion.

A leprous man lives outside the camp so…

This Torah Portion teaches me…

....

....

....

....

Metzora

ad Leviticus 14:1-15:33. Write a summary of this Torah Portion.

....

....

....

1. What did a cleansed man do before he re-entered the camp?

....

....

2. Where did this man live for seven days?

....

....

3. What did this man take to the priest on the 8th day?

....

....

Draw your favorite scene from this Torah Portion.

Yah used the priests to…	This Torah Portion teaches me…
....	....
....	....

Acharei Mot

Read Leviticus 16:1-18:30. Write a summary of this Torah Portion.

....

....

....

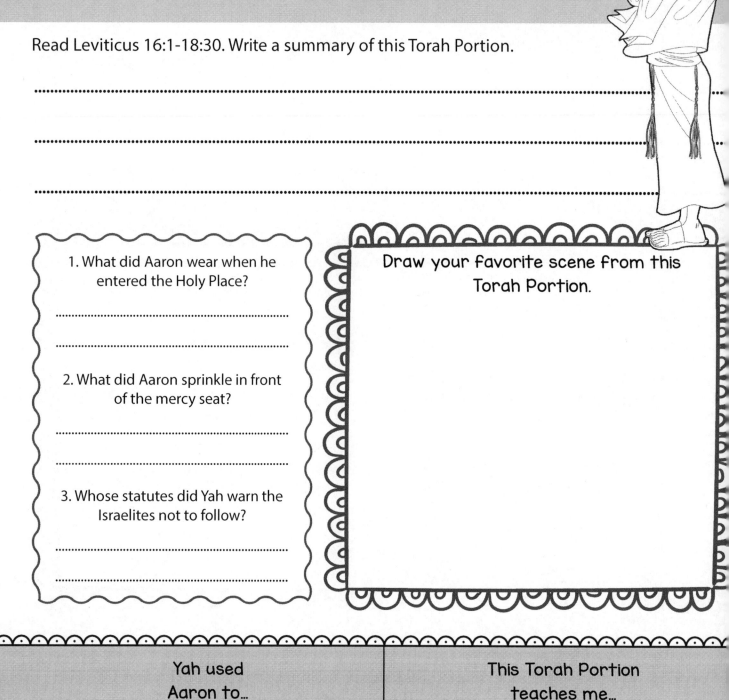

1. What did Aaron wear when he entered the Holy Place?

....

....

2. What did Aaron sprinkle in front of the mercy seat?

....

....

3. Whose statutes did Yah warn the Israelites not to follow?

....

....

Draw your favorite scene from this Torah Portion.

Yah used Aaron to…

....

....

This Torah Portion teaches me…

....

....

Kedoshim

ad Leviticus 19:1-20:27. Write a summary of this Torah Portion.

....

....

....

1. What should we not make out of cast metal?

....
....

2. What should we not do to our bodies?

....
....

3. Who should we honor in Leviticus 19:32?

....
....

Draw your favorite scene from this Torah Portion.

It's important to honor older people because…

....
....

This Torah Portion teaches me…

....
....

Emor

Read Leviticus 21:1-24:23. Write a summary of this Torah Portion.

....

....

....

1. Which Feast takes place seven weeks after First Fruits?

....

....

2. On what day is the Day of Trumpets?

....

....

3. What do Israelites dwell in during the Feast of Sukkot?

....

....

Draw your favorite scene from this Torah Portion.

Keeping Yah's Feasts is important because…

....

....

This Torah Portion teaches me…

....

....

Behar

Read Leviticus 25:1-26:2. Write a summary of this Torah Portion.

....

....

....

1. What is the fiftieth year to the Israelites?

....

....

2. How should we treat a brother who becomes poor?

....

....

3. Who should not be sold as slaves?

....

....

Draw your favorite scene from this Torah Portion.

If we obey Yah's instructions, He promises to...

This Torah Portion teaches me...

....

....

....

....

Bechukotai

Read Leviticus 26:3-27:34. Write a summary of this Torah Portion.

....

....

....

1. How long will the grape harvest last?

....

....

2. Where will Yah scatter His people?

....

....

3. What is the value of a man
20 - 60 years old?

....

....

Draw your favorite scene from this
Torah Portion.

If the people obeyed Yah's
instructions, He promised to...

This Torah Portion
teaches me...

....

....

....

....

B'midbar

Read Numbers 1:1-4:20. Write a summary of this Torah Portion.

....

....

....

1. What instructions did Yah give Moses?

....

....

2. Whose job was it to carry the Ark of the Covenant?

....

....

3. Who were Aaron's four sons?

....

....

Draw your favorite scene from this Torah Portion.

Yah used the Levites to…	This Torah Portion teaches me…
....	....
....	....

Nasso

Read Numbers 4:21-7:89. Write a summary of this Torah Portion.

....

....

....

1. For how long can a Nazarite not cut his hair?

....

....

2. What gift does a Nazarite bring Yah after he has finished his vow?

....

....

3. Where can a Nazarite shave his head?

....

....

Draw your favorite scene from this Torah Portion.

Read Judges 13:5.
Yah used Samson to...

....

....

This Torah Portion teaches me...

....

....

Beha'alotcha

Read Numbers 8:1-12:16. Write a summary of this Torah Portion.

....

....

....

1. How many lamps give light in front of the menorah?

....

....

2. How long did a Levite serve in the Tabernacle?

....

....

3. Why did Yah sent fire among parts of the camp?

....

....

Draw your favorite scene from this Torah Portion.

I keep the Passover meal because...

....

....

This Torah Portion teaches me...

....

....

Shelach Lecha

Read Numbers 13:1-15:41. Write a summary of this Torah Portion.

....

....

....

1. How many men went to spy out Canaan?

....

....

2. Who did the spies see in the Negev?

....

....

3. How long did the spies stay in Canaan?

....

....

Draw your favorite scene from this Torah Portion.

List the people in your family who wear tzitzits.

....

....

This Torah Portion teaches me...

....

....

Korach

ad Numbers 16:1-18:32. Write a summary of this Torah Portion.

....

....

....

1. Whose authority did Korah and the men challenge?

....

....

2. What happened to Korah's men and their households?

....

....

3. What killed 14,700 people in the camp?

....

....

Draw your favorite scene from this Torah Portion.

Yah punished Korah and his men because...

....

....

This Torah Portion teaches me...

....

....

Chukat

Read Numbers 19:1-22:1. Write a summary of this Torah Portion.

....

....

....

1. Where did Miriam die?

....

....

2. What happened when Moses struck the rock twice?

....

....

3. Why did Yah send fiery serpents among the Israelites?

....

....

Draw your favorite scene from this Torah Portion.

Yah used Moses to…

....

....

This Torah Portion teaches me…

....

....

Balak

Read Numbers 22:2-25:9. Write a summary of this Torah Portion.

....

....

....

1. Why did Balak ask Balaam to come to Moab?

....

....

2. What animal spoke to Balaam?

....

....

3. How many times did Balaam bless the Israelites?

....

....

Draw your favorite scene from this Torah Portion.

Yah used Balaam to…

....

....

This Torah Portion teaches me…

....

....

Pinchas

Read Numbers 25:10-30:1. Write a summary of this Torah Portion.

....

....

....

1. What covenant did Yah give Phinehas?

....

....

2. Why did Yah not let Moses enter the Promised Land?

....

....

3. Who did Yah anoint as leader after Moses?

....

....

Draw your favorite scene from this Torah Portion.

Which Feasts do we bring offerings before Yah?

....

....

This Torah Portion teaches me...

....

....

Matot

Read Numbers 30:2-32:42. Write a summary of this Torah Portion.

....

....

....

1. Who were the five kings of Midian?

....

....

2. Who led the battle against the Midianites?

....

....

3. How many donkeys were taken from the Midianites?

....

....

Draw your favorite scene from this Torah Portion.

Yah used Phinehas to…	This Torah Portion teaches me…

Masei

Read Numbers 33:1-36:13. Write a summary of this Torah Portion.

....

....

....

1. Who led the Israelites out of Egypt?

....

....

2. What did the Israelites find at Elim?

....

....

3. What is the punishment for murder?

....

....

Draw your favorite scene from this Torah Portion.

Yah established cities of refuge because…

....

....

This Torah Portion teaches me…

....

....

D'varim

Read Deuteronomy 1:1-3:22. Write a summary of this Torah Portion.

....

....

....

1. Why were the Israelites afraid to enter the Promised Land?

....

....

2. How many years did the Israelites live in the wilderness?

....

....

3. How big was King Og's bed?

....

....

Draw your favorite scene from this Torah Portion.

An Israelite is someone who…	This Torah Portion teaches me…

Va'etchanan

Read Deuteronomy 3:23-7:11. Write a summary of this Torah Portion.

....

....

....

1. On what did Yah write the Ten Commandments?

....

....

2. Why did Yah let the Israelites hear His voice from heaven?

....

....

3. What seven nations did the Israelites defeat?

....

....

Draw your favorite scene from this Torah Portion.

Yah used Moses to teach the…

....

....

This Torah Portion teaches me…

....

....

Eikev

ead Deuteronomy 7:12-11:25. Write a summary of this Torah Portion.

....

....

....

1. What did Yah feed the Israelites in the wilderness?

....

....

2. What did Moses do to the golden calf?

....

....

3. What will happen if the Israelites worship other gods?

....

....

Draw your favorite scene from this Torah Portion.

The Israelites lived in the wilderness for forty years so...

This Torah Portion teaches me...

....

....

....

....

Re'eh

Read Deuteronomy 11:26-16:17. Write a summary of this Torah Portion.

....

....

....

1. What did Yah set before the Israelites?

....

....

2. What should you not boil in its mother's milk?

....

....

3. How long is the Feast of Sukkot?

....

....

Draw your favorite scene from this Torah Portion.

I keep the Feast of Sukkot by…

....

....

This Torah Portion teaches me…

....

....

Shoftim

ead Deuteronomy 16:18-21:9. Write a summary of this Torah Portion.

....

....

....

1. What should judges not accept?

....

....

2. What four things should a king not acquire?

....

....

3. What is an abomination to Yah?

....

....

Draw your favorite scene from this Torah Portion.

I should avoid the occult because…

....

....

This Torah Portion teaches me…

....

....

Ki Teitzei

Read Deuteronomy 21:10-25:19. Write a summary of this Torah Portion.

....

....

....

1. What will happen to a rebellious son?

....

....

2. How long can a newly married man spend time with his wife at home?

....

....

3. On what day should you pay a hired worker?

....

....

Draw your favorite scene from this Torah Portion.

I treat people with respect by…

....

....

This Torah Portion teaches me…

....

....

Ki Tavo

Read Deuteronomy 26:1-29:8. Write a summary of this Torah Portion.

....

....

....

1. Which year is the year of tithing?

....

....

2. What will happen if the Israelites obey Yah's commandments?

....

....

3. Where did Yah make a covenant with the Israelites?

....

....

Draw your favorite scene from this Torah Portion.

Yah used Moses to…	This Torah Portion teaches me…

Nitzavim

Read Deuteronomy 29:9-30:20. Write a summary of this Torah Portion.

....

....

....

1. With whom did Yah make
   a covenant?

....

....

2. Which cities did Yah overthrow?

....

....

3. What will happen if we serve
   other gods?

....

....

Draw your favorite scene from this
Torah Portion.

If we obey His instructions,
Yah promises to…

This Torah Portion
teaches me…

.... | ....

.... | ....

Vayelech

Read Deuteronomy 31:1-30. Write a summary of this Torah Portion.

....

....

....

1. How old was Moses when he spoke to the Israelites?

....

....

2. What shall be read to the Israelites at Sukkot?

....

....

3. What did Moses tell the Levites to put by the Ark?

....

....

Draw your favorite scene from this Torah Portion.

Yah used the Levites to…	This Torah Portion teaches me…

Ha'azinu

Read Deuteronomy 32:1-52. Write a summary of this Torah Portion.

....

....

....

1. How did the Israelites make Yah angry?

....

....

2. On which mountain did Aaron die?

....

....

3. What city is mentioned in verse 49?

....

....

Draw your favorite scene from this Torah Portion.

I can please Yah by…

....

....

This Torah Portion teaches me…

....

....

V'Zot HaBerachah

Read Deuteronomy 33:1-34:12. Write a summary of this Torah Portion.

....

....

....

1. From where did Yah shine forth?

....

....

2. Who crouches like a lion?

....

....

3. How old was Moses when he died?

....

....

Draw your favorite scene from this Torah Portion.

Obeying Yah's Torah is important because…	This Torah Portion teaches me…
....	....
....	....

Bereshit Weekly Torah Study Guide

With readings from the Prophets and the Apostles

Parashah	Torah Reading	Prophets' Reading	Apostles' Reading
Bereshit	Genesis 1:1-6:8	Isaiah 42:5-43:10	John 1:1-18
			Romans 5:12-21
			Matthew 19:4-6
Noach	Genesis 6:9-11:32	Isaiah 54:1-55:5	Matthew 24:36-44
			1 Peter 3:18-22
Lech-Lecha	Genesis 12:1-17:27	Isaiah 40:27-41:16	Hebrews 7:1-22
			Romans 4:1-25
			Acts 7:1-8
Vayeira	Genesis 18:1-22:24	2 Kings 4:1-37	Galatians 4:21-31
			James 2:14-24
			Hebrews 11:13-19
Chayei Sarah	Genesis 23:1-25:18	1 Kings 1:1-31	1 Peter 3:1-7
			1 Cor 15:50-57
			Hebrews 11:11-16
Toledot	Genesis 25:19-28:9	Malachi 1:1-2:7	Romans 9:6-16
			Hebrews 11:20 & 12:14-17
Vayetze	Genesis 28:10-32:3	Hosea 12:12-14:9	Mark 1:16-20
			John 1:43-51
			Hebrews 8:6-8
Vayishlach	Genesis 32:3-36:43	Hosea 11:7-12:12	Matthew 26:36-46
			Revelation 7:1-14
			1 Corinthians 5:1-13
Vayeshev	Genesis 37:1-40:23	Amos 2:6-3:8	Acts 7:9-16
Miketz	Genesis 41:1-44:17	1 Kings 3:15-4:1	Matthew 7:2
			Acts 7:9-16
Vayigash	Genesis 44:18-47:27	Ezekiel 37:15-28	Romans 9:1-19
			Romans 11:13-24
			Ephesians 2:11-22
			Matthew 10:1-7, 34
Vayechi	Genesis 47:28-50:26	1 Kings 2:1-12	1 Peter 2:4-10
			Luke 1:23-33
			Hebrews 11:21-22

Shemot Weekly Torah Study Guide

With readings from the Prophets and the Apostles

arashah	Torah Reading	Prophets' Reading	Apostles' Reading
hemot	Exodus 1:1-6:1	Isaiah 27:6–28:13; 29:22-23	Hebrews 11:23-27
			Acts 7:17-35
			Luke 20:37
a'eira	Exodus 6:2-9:35	Ezekiel 28:25–29:21	Romans 9:14–17
			Acts 7:7,17–35
			1 Cor 3:11–15
o	Exodus 10:1-13:16	Jeremiah 46:13-28	John 19:1-37
			Acts 13:16-17
			2 Cor 6:14-7:1
eshalach	Exodus 13:17-17:16	Judges 4:4-5:31	1 Cor 10:1-13
			Revelation 15:1-4
			Romans 9:15-23
itro	Exodus 18:1-20:26	Isaiah 6:1-7:6, 9:6-7	Matthew 19:16-30
			1 Timothy 3:1-3
			James 2:8-13
Mishpatim	Exodus 21:1-24:18	Jeremiah 34:8-22, 33:25-26	James 3:2-12
			Matthew 5:38-42
			Hebrews 12:25-29
erumah	Exodus 25:1-27:19	1 Kings 5:26-5:13	Hebrews 13:10-12
			Matthew 5:14-16
			Hebrews 10:19-22
etzaveh	Exodus 27:20-30:10	Ezekiel 43:10-27	Hebrews 5:1-10
			Hebrews 13:10-17
			Romans 12:1
i Tisa	Exodus 30:11-34:35	1 Kings 18:1-39	1 Cor 12:1-31
			Acts 7:39-42
			Hebrews 3:1-6
ayakhel	Exodus 35:1-38:20	1 Kings 7:13-26, 40-50	Hebrews 9:1-28
			2 Cor 9:1-15
			Hebrews 10:26-31
ekudei	Exodus 38:21-40:38	1 Kings 7:51-8:21	1 Cor 3:1-17
			Hebrews 5:1-11
			Hebrews 7:1-8:6

Vayikra Weekly Torah Study Guide

With readings from the Prophets and the Apostles

Parashah	Torah Reading	Prophets' Reading	Apostles' Reading
Vayikra	Leviticus 1:1-5:26	Isaiah 43:21-44:23	Romans 8:1-13
			Hebrews 9:11-28
			Hebrews 10:1-22
Tzav	Leviticus 6:1-8:36	Jeremiah 7:21-8:3,	Ephesians 6:10-18
		Jeremiah 9:22(23)-23(24)	2 Cor 6:14-7:1
			Hebrews 10:1-39
Shemini	Leviticus 9:1-11:47	2 Samuel 6:1-7:17	Acts 5:1-11
			1 Timothy 3:1-13
			1 Peter 1:14-16
Tazria	Leviticus 12:1-13:59	2 Kings 4:42-5:19	Luke 2:22-24
			Mark 1:40-45
			James 3:1-12
Metzora	Leviticus 14:1-15:33	2 Kings 7:3-20	Matthew 9:20-26
			Romans 6:19-23
			1 Peter 1:15-16
Acharei Mot	Leviticus 16:1-18:30	Ezekiel 22:1-19	Hebrews 7:11-10:22
			Matthew 27:5
			Ephesians 1:5-7
Kedoshim	Leviticus 19:1-20:27	Amos 9:7-15	Ephesians 6:1-3
		Ezekiel 20:2-20	Ephesians 4:24-32
			Matthew 5:43-48
Emor	Leviticus 21:1-24:23	Ezekiel 44:15-31	1 Peter 1:13-17
			Matthew 5:38-42
			James 2:1-9
Behar	Leviticus 25:1-26:2	Jeremiah 32:6-27	1 Cor 7:21-24
			Galatians 6:7-10
			Luke 4:16-21
Bechukotai	Leviticus 26:3-27:34	Jeremiah 16:19-17:14	Matthew 7:21-27
			Colossians 3:1-10
			John 14:15-2

B'midbar Weekly Torah Study Guide

With readings from the Prophets and the Apostles

arashah	Torah Reading	Prophets' Reading	Apostles' Reading
'midbar	Numbers 1:1-4:20	Hosea 2:1(1:10) - 2:22(20)	Revelation 7:1-8
			Revelation 4:1-11
			Titus 1:5-9
asso	Numbers 4:21-7:89	Judges 13:2-25	Mark 1:40-45
			Acts 21:17-26
			John 8:1-11
eha'alotcha	Numbers 8:1-12:16	Zechariah 2:10 (14)-4:7	Hebrews 4:14-5:10
			Hebrews 7:1-28
			1 Corinthians 10:10
helach Lecha	Numbers 13:1-15:41	Joshua 2:1-24	Hebrews 3:7-19
			Ephesians 2:11-19
			Galatians 3:28-29
orach	Numbers 16:1-18:32	1 Samuel 11:14-12:22	Jude 1-25
			John 15:1-7
			1 Timothy 5:17-18
hukat	Numbers 19:1-22:1	Judges 11:1-33	John 3:9-21
			Hebrews 9:11-22
			1 Corinthians 15:55-57
alak	Numbers 22:2-25:9	Micah 5:6-6:8	2 Peter 2:1-22
			Jude 11
			Revelation 2:14-15
inchas	Numbers 25:10-30:1	1 Kings 18:46-19:21	1 Timothy 3:2-7
			2 Peter 2:14-22
			Romans 12:1
Matot	Numbers 30:2-32:42	Jeremiah 1:1-2:3	Matthew 5:33-37
			Ephesians 5:21-33
Masei	Numbers 33:1-36:13	Jeremiah 2:4-28 & 3:4	Ephesians 6:10-18
			James 4:1-12
			2 Corinthians 10:3-6

D'varim Weekly Torah Study Guide

With readings from the Prophets and the Apostles

Parashah	Torah Reading	Prophets' Reading	Apostles' Reading
D'varim	Deuteronomy 1:1-3:22	Isaiah 1:1-27	James 2:1-9
			Acts 7:38-45
			Hebrews 3:7-4:11
Va'etchanan	Deuteronomy 3:23-7:11	Isaiah 40:1-26	Romans 1:18-25
			Mark 12:28-34
			1 Corinthians 6:19-20
Eikev	Deuteronomy 7:12-11:25	Isaiah 49:14-51:3	Hebrews 12:5-11
			Romans 8:31-39
			1 John 2:3-5
Re'eh	Deuteronomy 11:26-16:17	Isaiah 44:11-45:5	1 Corinthians 5:9-13
			2 Peter 2:1-22
			Hebrews 4:1-10
Shoftim	Deuteronomy 16:18-21:9	Isaiah 51:12-53:12	Hebrews 10:28-31
			1 Timothy 5:17-22
			Acts 7:35-53
Ki Teitzei	Deuteronomy 21:10-25:19	Isaiah 54:1-10	Luke 10:29-37
			1 Corinthians 11:2-15
			Mark 10:2-12
Ki Tavo	Deuteronomy 26:1-29:8	Isaiah 60:1-22	Romans 2:6-11
			Luke 21:1-4
			1 John 2:3-6
Nitzavim	Deuteronomy 29:9-30:20	Isaiah 61:10-63:9	Romans 10:6-8
			John 10:1-5
			Hebrews 8:7-12
Vayelech	Deuteronomy 31:1-30	Isaiah 55:6-56:8	Hebrews 13:5
			Romans 8:31, 37
			Hebrews 8:7-12
Ha'azinu	Deuteronomy 32:1-52	2 Samuel 22:1-51	Romans 9:24-29
			Revelation 3:14-21
			Matthew 10:5-6
V'Zot HaBerachah	Deuteronomy 33:1-34:12	Joshua 1:1-18	Acts 3:22-23
			Hebrews 3:5
			Acts 7:17-44

eshit
Sixth day
Adam
930 years old

ach
Seven
A rainbow
To the heavens

h-Lecha
Because Sarah was living in Pharaoh's house
Abram fought to save Lot
A son called Isaac

eira
Sarah
Fire and sulfur (brimstone) out of heaven
To offer Isaac as a burnt offering

ayei Sarah
In the cave of the field of Machpelah
A gold ring, two bracelets, gold and silver jewelry, and garments
Isaac, son of Abraham

edot
Jacob and Esau
Because Isaac was very wealthy – he had many servants and flocks and herds of animals
Jacob was afraid Esau might kill him

etze
Angels of Yah
Seven years + seven years
In her camel's saddle

ishlach
Four hundred men
Yah told Jacob, "For you have striven with God and men and prevailed."
They had too many possessions to dwell together. The land could not support them because of all their livestock

Vayeshev
1. Potifar
2. Cupbearer and baker
3. The Pharaoh

Miketz
1. Governor of Egypt (Gen 42:6)
2. To buy grain
3. Silver cup

Vayigash
1. The best land in Egypt
2. Land of Goshen
3. Food

Vayechi
1. Manasseh
2. Issachar
3. Seventy days

Shemot
1. Kill the Hebrew baby boys and let the Hebrew baby girls live
2. Land of Midian
3. He made the Hebrews gather their own straw to make bricks

Va'eira
1. Abraham, Isaac, and Jacob
2. The Egyptians' livestock
3. Land of Goshen

Bo
1. Abib
2. Forever
3. Death of firstborn

Beshalach
1. Joseph's bones
2. By a strong wind
3. He told Moses to strike the rock with his staff, and water gushed forth

Yitro
1. Moses' father-in-law
2. Mount Sinai
3. The Sabbath

Mishpatim
1. Let it rest and do not plant crops
2. Unleavened Bread
3. Unleavened Bread (Matzah), Harvest (Shavuot), and Tabernacles (Sukkot)

Terumah
1. Acacia wood
2. The testimony (stone tablets with the commandments inscribed on them)
3. Gold

Tetzaveh
1. Aaron, Nadab, and Abihu
2. Twelve stones
3. Blue

Ki Tisa
1. A calf
2. Melted it in the fire and ground it to dust
3. He forced them to drink gold dust

Vayakhel
1. Skilled craftsmen
2. Seven branches
3. Bronze

Pekudei
1. Twenty-nine talents and 730 shekels
2. At the entrance of the Tabernacle
3. The cloud of Yah was on the Tabernacle by day and fire in it by night

Vayikra
1. To a priest at the entrance of the Tabernacle
2. Turtledoves or pigeons
3. Bull

Tzav
1. The priest who offers it
2. At the entrance of the Tabernacle
3. The Urim and the Thummim

Shemini
1. Nadab and Abihu
2. Unauthorized fire which He had not commanded them
3. They were consumed by fire

Tazria
1. The priest
2. Torn clothing
3. Outside the camp

Metzora
1. Wash his clothes, shave off all his hair, and bathe in water
2. In the camp but outside his tent
3. Two male lambs without blemish, one ewe lamb without blemish, and a grain offering

Acharei Mot
1. The garments of the high priest (holy linen coat, linen undergarment, linen sash and linen turban)
2. Bull's blood
3. Egyptians and Canaanites

Kedoshim
1. False gods
2. Make cuts on our body for the dead or tattoo ourselves
3. Older people

Emor
1. Shavuot (Pentecost)
2. First day of the seventh month
3. Sukkahs (temporary shelters)

Behar
1. A Jubilee
2. Support him as though he were a stranger and a sojourner, take no interest or profit from him, and do not lend him money at interest or give him food for profit
3. The Israelites

Bechukotai
1. Until the time for sowing
2. Among the nations
3. Fifty shekels of silver

B'midbar
1. Take a census of all the congregation of Israel
2. The Levites
3. Nadab, Abihu, Eleazar, and Ithamar

Nasso
1. All the days of his vow of separation
2. One male lamb, a year old without blemish, one ewe lamb year old without blemish, and a basket of unleavened bread
3. At the entrance to the tabernacle

Beha'alotcha
1. Seven lamps
2. Twenty-five years
3. Because the Israelites complained

ach Lecha
Twelve men – one from each tribe of Israel
The descendants of Anak (the Nephilim)
Forty days

ach
Moses and Aaron
The earth swallowed up the men and their households
A plague

kat
Kadesh
Water poured out of the rock
Because the Israelites kept complaining

k
To curse the Israelites
A donkey
Balaam blessed the Israelites three times

has
Covenant of peace
Because Moses did not uphold Yah as holy at the waters of Meribah
Joshua

ot
Evi, Rekem, Zur, Hur, and Reva
Phinehas
61,000 donkeys

ei
Moses and Aaron
Twelve springs and seventy palm trees
Death

arim
Because the cities and people were bigger than the Israelites, and the sons of Anakim lived there
Forty years
Nine cubits long and four cubits wide

tchanan
Two stone tablets
So that He might discipline the Israelites
The Hittites, the Girgashites, the Amorites, the Canaanites, the Perizzites, the Hivites, and the Jebusites

Eikev
1. Manna and quail
2. Burned it with fire, crushed it, ground it until it was like fine dust, and threw the dust into the stream
3. The Israelites will perish

Re'eh
1. A blessing and a curse
2. A young goat
3. Seven days

Shoftim
1. Bribes
2. Many horses, wives, and excessive silver and gold
3. Witchcraft and divination (the occult)

Ki Teitzei
1. He will be stoned to death by the men of the city
2. One year
3. On the same day he has worked, before sunset

Ki Tavo
1. Third year
2. They will be blessed and set high above the nations
3. Horeb

Nitzavim
1. The people of Israel
2. Sodom and Gomorrah, Admah, and Zeboiim
3. You will perish and not live long in the land

Vayelech
1. Moses was 120 years old
2. The Torah
3. Book of the Law

Ha'azinu
1. By worshipping other gods
2. Nebo
3. Jericho

V'Zot HaBerachah
1. Mount Paran
2. Gad
3. Moses was 120 years' old

◇◇ **Discover more Activity Books!** ◇◇

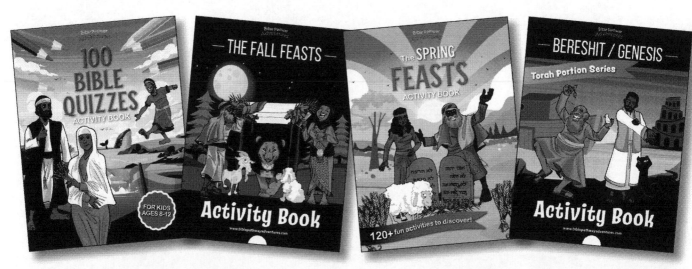

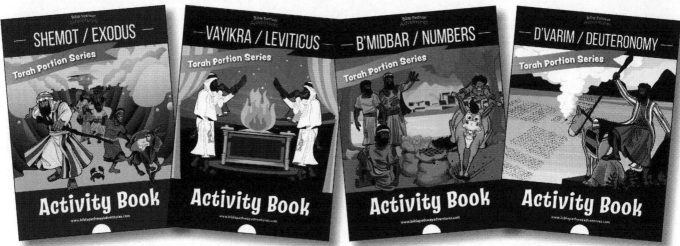

Available for purchase at www.biblepathwayadventures.com

INSTANT DOWNLOAD!

100 Bible Quizzes	Shemot / Exodus
The Fall Feasts	Vayikra / Leviticus
The Spring Feasts	B'midbar / Numbers
Bereshit / Genesis	D'varim / Deuteronomy

Made in United States
Troutdale, OR
11/03/2024